W9-CEA-494

桂林山水
Guilin's Landscape

摄影: 简 亮　　JIAN LIANG

 羊城晚报 出版社

· 广 州 ·

桂林之夜　　The Night of Guilin
桂林の夜　　桂林의 석양으로 가는 노래가릭

象鼻山
The Elephant Hill

象鼻山
상비산

象山又名漓山、沉水山。酷似在江边吸水的大象，故又名象鼻山。它被誉为桂林的城徽，盛名远扬。
The Elephant Hill is also called Li Hill and Chengshui Hill. Resembling an elephant drinking water from the river, it is also called Elephant Trunk Hill. It is called as the emblem of Guilin and its fame spreads far and wide.

山村小景　A scenic spot at a mountain village　山村のながめ　산촌의 풍경

骆驼山峰　　　　　骆驼山
Camel Hill in Autumn　낙타산

又名酒壶山，形似骆驼，遂名骆驼山，相传雷酒人曾在此酿酒成仙，为桂林八景之一。
Also known as kettle Hill. For it looks like a camel, it`s also called Camel Hill. Legend says that a drunk man named Lei drank here and became immortal. It is one of the eight scenes of Guilin.

霞光万道　　　霞
Splendid sunset　여러갈래의 노을빛

群峰梦醒　Sunshine on cloudy mountains　奇峰の夜明　곰속에서 깨여난 수천봉우리

木龙古渡　　　木龍の古い渡り
The ancient ferry at Mulong　목룡옛나루터

水上人家　　　水上生活
Family boats on the River　水上의人家

秀水奇山
Beautiful waters borders on wonderful hills

奇山と清き水
기이한산수려한물

伏波山伫立在桂林城漓江边，有镇南伏波大将军在山下一剑斩石、箭射穿山定边界及稚童还珠等美好的传说。
The wave Taming Hill stands beside the Li River in the city. It has beautiful legends such as Fubo general cutting a rock at the foot of the hill by a sword and shooting an arrow piercing the Tunnel Hill defining the boundary, and young boy returning the pearl.

瑞　雪　　瑞兆の雪
Timely snow　첫 눈

穿山、塔山隔江相对，活像一对大公鸡相斗，栩栩如生，俗称斗鸡山。这里景色秀丽，位于城东，是市民休闲的好去处。
The Tunnel Hill and Pagoda Hill stand oppositely across the river, just like two cocks fighting against each other.
It is very true to life and is called Game Cock Hills. The scenery here in the east part of the city is beautiful and
it is a good place for the citizens to go for recreation.

南溪山　　南溪山
South Stream Hill　남계산

南溪山位于桂林城南门，这里的名胜古迹很多，有白龙桥、白龙洞、泗渊岩、刘仙岩等著名景观。
The South Stream Hill locates in the south of city. It abounds in scenic spots and his torical sites, in cluding the White Dragon Bridge, White Dragon Cave, Siyuan Cave and Immortal Liu Cave and so on.

山乡之春　　　山里の春

A mountain village in spring　산간의 봄

奇峰镇位于桂林城南 10 千米处，这里山峰奇特、怪石连陈，群山环绕大片沃土，是摄影家的乐园。
The Strange Peak Town locates 10Km to south of Guilin city. Here the peaks are peculiar and strange rocks are rolling and group of hills surround vast expanses of fertile land. It is a paradise for photographers.

山在虚无飘渺间　　霧 に 包 ま れ る 峰 々
Hills in a Celestial Land　산들이　희미하게　드러나다

漓江梦幻
Lijiang River in a dream
灘江夢幻
리강의 봉한

群峰竞秀
The green hills rise sharply and
compete each other for beauty
群峰ガ秀逸を競う
아름다움올 다투는 뭇봉우리

水车 Water wheel 水車 수차

尧山杜鹃　　らん漫たる山花
Azaleas in Yao Hill　　산 꽃이　난만하다

东郊尧山是桂林城区最大的山脉，有方圆100多千米的靖江王墓群，尧山瑞雪是桂林八大景之首，三月遍开杜鹃花。
Mt Yao in the east suburb is the largest mountain in Giulin. There are Jingjiang Prince Tombs which occupy an area of over 100Km2. The snow on Mt Yao is the first of the eight scenes of Guilin. In March, azaleas bloom all over the mountain.

晨光之影　　　　曉に浴びる山水
Light and Reflections　아침햇살을　감수하고　있는　山水

漓江中游浪石村边的风景远观近看，处处奇绝，相传为二郎神的鬼斧神工所造。
The scenery beside the Waving Stone Village on the Middle of Li River is so wonderful that no matter viewed from near or afar. It is said that is was built with the axe of Erlang spirit.

浪石风光　　　浪石の風光
A beautiful scene of Langshi　랑석풍광

下龙风光 下龍の風光
A wonderful scene of Xialong 하룡의 풍광

漓江下龙村一带景色秀丽，山峰奇特，最具"桂林山水甲天下"诗意的造形。
The scenery at the xialong Village on the bank of Li River is beautiful and the hills and peaks here best embodies the poem "Guilin`s water and mountain are the best under heaven."

画山牧牛
Tending Cattle Beside a Mural Hill

九匹つ馬が山をえがく
구 마 화 산

山形似九马，栩栩如生，故有民谣："问你神马有几匹？看出九匹中状元。"
The shape of the hill is like nine horses, hence the folk rhyme goes: "How many horses can you tell?
If you can name nine of them all out you are sure to be NO.1 Scholar in the world."

鸟瞰黄布滩　　　灘江を鳥瞰する

Sunshine over Li River　　漓江의 概观

黄布滩两岸有七个山峰浴水而出，传说是七仙女迷恋漓江不返天宫而被化为石峰。
At the yellow Cloth Shoal on the banks of the Li River, there are seven peaks. Legend has it that they were turned from seven fairies who were infatuated with the Li River`s scenery of and were reluctant to return to the heavenly court and were turned into stone hills.

漓江红帆　　灕江紅帆

Red Sail on the Li River　漓江의 붉은 돛배

奇峰倒影，滴翠如油，红帆点点若隐若现，撼人心魄。
The strange peaks reflect on the water, the lush green
and the dots of red sails, The sene is thrilling.

雨后新虹　雨后の虹
Rainbow　비그친 뒤 무지개

朝笏山
Chao Ban Hill
[朝板]山
朝板山

漓江秀色　　　灘江の美しい姿
Beautiful Li River　이강의 아름다운 경치

兴坪是漓江渔民的聚居地，这里山峰酷似骆驼过江，20元人民币图案由此景绘制而出。
Xingping is place where fishermen live in compact community, One peak here looks like a camel crossing the river, The design on the 20-Yuan bill of RMB contains a drawing of this scene.

螺丝山牧牛
Returnign Home Afttle Grazing

川のほとりに牛を放牧する
강가의　소떼

兴坪是漓江中游最大的古镇，这里两岸翠竹成阴，山峦秀丽，是徒步游漓江的最佳歇息地。
Xingping is the largest ancient town on the middle reach of Li River, Here the green bamboo
is in grooves and hills are beautiful. An ideal place for rest for Li River pedestrian travelers.

群峰倒影山浮山
Inverted Images of Peaks Floating in the Water

峰峰の倒影は水に浮ぶ
여러 봉우리 물에 비치니 산은 물우에 버있는 듯

春江水暖鸭先知
Ducks are the first to know the coming
of spring through their sense

川水暖く，鴨は先知る春の來たりし
봄물의 따뜻함은 오리가 먼저 알리니라

当你在漓江看到云雾氤氲，山峦葱翠的景观，当然是一种神仙般的享受。
The scene of green peaks amid dense fog on Li River makes
you feel like an immortal.

"一带山河　少年努力"石刻
Engraved Calligraphy　石刻［一帶山河　少年努力］
간하의　소녀들이여　정전하라—— 석각

碧莲峰下住人家　　碧蓮峰の麓に住む民家
Homes by the Lotus Hill　碧莲峰아래의　농가

书童山红叶　　　　秋色に書童
Red Maple Leaves on Scholar`s Hill　서동의　수려한　풍경

俗称桅杆山。山腰裂出一石，形如拱立的女装男童，名书童山。对岸的山名秀才看榜，名落孙山的秀才一直没有看到自己的名字。
Also called Mast Hill. At the mountain side there is a rock resembling a pageboy, hence its name Page-Boy Hill.
The opposite hill is called Scholar Reading a Bulletin.

秋 韵

Concerto of Autumn

秋 の 雅趣

가을의 雅趣

放牛归家　　Returuing Home After Cattle Tending　　牧人の歸り　　방목하고 돌아오는 질

山水之情
Sunset Along the Lijiang River
灘水情
漓江의 情

桂林山甲天下，阳朔堪称甲桂林，群峰倒影山浮水，无水无山不入神。
The landscape of Guilin is the best under heaven but Yangshuo is still the better. Group of
hills float inverted in the water, hills setting off by water make the scene even charmer.

漓江秋韵　The autumn lingering charm of Lijiang River　灕江の秋色　리강의　아름다운　가을경치

月亮山　月光の山
Moon Hill　월량산

月亮山，山上有一洞似月亮，边走边看月牙形状也随山形改变而变化，真是"月亮走呀我也走"。
The Moon Hill, on the hill there is a cave liks a moon, The shape of the moon changes from crescent to full when you walk passing the hill.

大榕树
Great Banyan

大きい古榕
용나무

大榕树盘根错节，叶茂蔽天，相传是刘三姐抛绣球给情郎的地方。
The Big Banyan tree has twisted roots and gnarled branches and dense leaves covring up the sky.
Legend has it that it is a place where Liusanjie threw embroidry ball, a pledge for love to her lover.

光　韵　　　曉に浴びる山水
Birth of the Sun　아침햇살을 감수하고 있는 山水

百寿石刻　　　　　百壽岩の石刻
Stone carving in Baishou Rock　백수암　석각

芦笛岩是大自然的艺术之宫
Ludi(Reed Flute) Cave-A Natural Art Palace

大自然芸術の宮 ― 蘆笛岩
대자연의　예술궁 ― 노적암

在滴水、流水飞溅的作用下使衍生物形成千姿百态的钟乳石奇观，仿佛进入人间仙境。
The marvelous spectacle of stalagmites in different shapes formed by the actions of dropping water and flowing water make you as if ener into an enrthly faiyland.

龙胜梯田   竜勝の棚田

Terraced Fields in Longsheng   용숭의 제전

从金坑大寨到小寨约 4 千米，山路崎岖需当地导游引路。
From Golden pit Big Village to Small Village, the road was rough.
The local guide guided the road.

晨光之韵　　夜明けの光り
A Cloudy morning　아침햇살

梯田景色千变万化，晨曦日出的光影，云绕山中的气氛都是不可多得的景观。
The scene of the terraced field is varied, among which the
sunrise and misty cloud are scenes.

瑞　雪　　　瑞兆の雪
Timely snow　　첫 눈

龙胜少数民族风情让您赏心悦目，糯米水酒、珍珠油茶、竹筒饭使您回味无穷。
The minority folk customs of Longsheng is pleasant. The glutinous rice
wine, pearl oil tea and bamboo tube rice will give you lingering tastes.

春到梯田　　段段ぱたけの春

Terraced Fields in Spring　고전의 봄

瑶山气候偏冷，梯田春插一般在五月底六月初，90天成熟，春插秋收各有特色，请别错过好时机。
The weather in Yao Hill is reletively cold, The terrace seedling transplant in spring is often done in end of May and beginning of June, The rice is ripe in 90 days.

鼓楼木屋　　トン族集落の鼓樓
Dong Log Cabins　풍족마윤의　고루

侗族每个寨子里都有一个鼓楼，均为木质结构，楼顶用多层瓦面建成金字塔造形，鼓楼是寨子聚会休闲场所。
In every Dong village, there is a drum-tower, which is all wood structures. The tower tops are made into a pyramid with layers of tiles. It is a place for meeting and entertainment.

恭城文武庙
The Confucian Temple in Gongcheng County
恭城の文寺
공성　문묘

千年古榕
A Thousand- Year-Old Banyan
ガジュマルの千年老木
천년 묵은 용수

月岭古村 "孝义可风" 坊　　月嶺古町の "孝義可風" と言う扁額
Ancient village of Yueling　　월령고촌의 '효의가풍' 비

湘山寺　Xiangshan Temple　山の寺　공성 문묘

富里古桥　　富裏のふる橋
The ancient bridge at Fuli　부리의 옛 다리

瑶寨风情　恋　歌
Folk Customs　풍속 세래

红瑶姑娘身上的盛装，据说要用一年手工才能绣织而成。
The jacket of hongyao girl, It is said that it can be woven for one year by hand

瑶山之春 Spring comes 山里の春 산간의 봄

风情 Folk Customs 恋歌 풍속세래

苗族 Miao People

瑶族 Yao People

侗族 Dong People

壮族 Zhuang People

秋 韵　　　　秋 の 雅趣
Concerto of Autumn　가을의 雅趣

海洋乡距桂林 35 千米，据说每棵银杏可养活一家人，秋天收获银杏后树叶转黄，远远望去真像一片黄色的海洋。
The Haiyang Town is 35Km away from Guilin. It is said that every gingko tree can support a family.
After reaping in autumn, the gingko trees turn yellow to form a yellow sea.

古桥新韵　New Charm of Old Bridge　山村 の 古橋　금강소교